**AIR UNIVERSITY**

**AIR FORCE DOCTRINE DEVELOPMENT AND
EDUCATION CENTER**

# The Airpower Advantage
# in Future Warfare
## *The Need for Strategy*

COLIN S. GRAY

Research Paper 2007-2

Originally published by the Airpower
Research Institute Maxwell Air Force Base,
Alabama 36112-6026

**Disclaimer**

Opinions, conclusions, and recommendations expressed or implied within are solely those of the author and do not necessarily represent the views of the Air Force Doctrine Development and Education Center (AFDDEC), Air University, the United States Air Force, the Department of Defense, or any other US Government agency. Cleared for public release: distribution unlimited.

# Contents

# About the Author

Dr. Colin S. Gray is Professor of International Politics and Strategic Studies at the University of Reading in England. He is a dual US-UK citizen and has served as an adviser in Washington and London. He was educated in England at the Universities of Manchester and Oxford. Dr. Gray has taught at universities in Britain, Canada, and the United States, has been assistant director of the International Institute for Strategic Studies (London), and worked with Herman Kahn at the Hudson Institute before founding the National Institute for Public Policy. From 1982 until 1987, he held a presidential appointment on the President's Advisory Committee on Arms Control and Disarmament.

Dr. Gray's work has addressed a wide range of subjects on national security. For example, he has written extensively on nuclear strategy, maritime strategy, space strategy, special operations, geopolitics, airpower, arms control, and strategic theory. He is the author of 22 books, including *Another Bloody Century: Future Warfare* (Phoenix, 2006); *Strategy and History: Essays on Theory and Practice* (Routledge, 2006); *War, Peace and International Relations: An Introduction to Strategic History (Routledge, 2007)*; and *Fighting Talk: Forty Maxims on War, Peace, and Strategy* (Praeger Security International, 2007). Currently, he is working on *The Strategy Bridge*, a major book on strategic theory.

# Summary

The United States has long suffered from a serious strategy deficit. For so long as Americans short change the strategic function, the leverage of US airpower must be much less than its potential. The study argues strongly for the rigorous application of strategic discipline to all airpower activity, not only the kinetic.

Even today, more than 100 years into the air age, many people are inappropriately committed to the view that either landpower or airpower must be the dominant force in warfare. In fact, extensive historical experience demonstrates that the relative utility of airpower is powerfully situational. Futurology is a necessary art, not science, but its record of prescience is poor. With respect to science and technology and to politics, our ability to see into the future is completely unreliable. Technical innovation lies at the heart of the case for privileging airpower in the American way of war, but such innovation comprises only one of warfare's seven vital contexts. The sheer complexity of war and warfare renders prediction, technological and other, a high-risk activity. The contexts of war and warfare are (1) political, (2) societal-cultural, (3) economic, (4) technological, (5) military-strategic, (6) geographical, and (7) historical.

The major purpose of the study is to contribute to some reduction in America's strategy deficit. A common and serious error is the belief that airpower theory is uniquely immature and contested. Currently, it so happens, literally every dimension of US military power is fraught with conceptual uncertainty. Specifically, landpower knows it is challenged by a transforming airpower; seapower is suffering from a conceptual and strategic crisis as it strives, in part, to reinvent itself for a world wherein it faces no first-class naval enemies, but in which it will have to devise effective answers to anti-access tactics by littoral states; spacepower and cyberwar are utterly bereft of strategic theory tailored for their realms of behavior; and nuclear weapons are almost in conceptual limbo, challenged by the radical improvements in precision conventional weapons. Airpower is in no better or worse condition than the others. In short, there is a general crisis of strategic comprehension, a lack of agreement on the most effective organizing ideas. Airpower is by no means lonely in suffering from strategic theoretical uncertainty.

The study argues that the United States needs a theory of war and warfare. It claims that future warfare will be diverse and that the tactical, operational, and strategic value of airpower must always be situational. A coherent theory of employment for all of airpower's capabilities, not only the kinetic, is needed. Airpower's potential utility lies within a spectrum of possibilities and is dependent on context.

Looking to the future, it would be an error to assume that the United States will enjoy the benefits of air dominance as of right. Capable enemies who have studied the US style in warfare would be hugely motivated to reduce the American airpower advantage. Such a reduction might be achieved not only by air defense but also by contesting the uses of space or cyberspace.

Near exclusive focus upon the contributions airpower can make to warfare is a mistake. Airpower will generate strategic effect in time of peace and crisis also. We should not forget the continuing relevance of the concept and attempted practice of deterrence.

The study advises frank recognition of airpower's situational limitations. Those limitations are less than they used to be, but some remain simply as a consequence of the physical realities of flight with reference to a conflict that must relate, ultimately, to decisions and behavior on land. It is necessary to acknowledge and exploit the technological, tactical, and operational fact that the balance of relative influence, at least in regular warfare, has shifted very noticeably in favor of airpower. Irregular warfare is another matter altogether, of course.

The discussion notes some important factors that can detract from airpower's effectiveness: for examples, poor air strategy, operational art, or tactics; inappropriate equipment; loss of vital support from space and cyberspace systems; performance by friendly landpower and seapower that is so poor that the military context is beyond rescue by the action of land-based airpower; and, last but not least, the harmful consequences of being directed by dysfunctional national policy and strategy.

The study reaches six conclusions:

1. The US asymmetric advantage in airpower must be exploited to the maximum.

2. It is necessary to be clear about the critical distinction between airpower as a war decider and as a war winner.

3. High technology is, and has to be, the American way in warfare. Much of the criticism of the American love affair with machines is simply irrelevant.

4. Unfortunately, the now long-standing debate between land-power and airpower over which is dominant in regular warfare is all too alive and well. This conflict is understandable, but it is thoroughly misconceived and continues to harm US military and strategic prowess.

5. It cannot be denied that people allow themselves, their affection, to be captured by their favorite machines. Again, this is understandable, but it is not helpful if airpower is to benefit from a genuinely strategic analysis and debate.

6. Only strategy has the potential to unlock the full leverage that the United States should expect to achieve through the threat and use of its multi-faceted airpower.

# The Airpower Advantage in Future Warfare

## The Need for Strategy

*Airpower has become the preferred American way of war.*

Grant T. Hammond, 2005

*Ultimately, the use of land power remains the most con-clusive instrument of strategy.*

Michael Evans, 2004

This is a study of strategy and of that most essential of concepts, strategic effect. If America is able to reduce or eliminate its strategy deficit, much of the argument that underlies analysis of the future roles and influence of airpower will fall away as irrelevant.[1] The strategic effect of airpower is the master theme that binds this work and to which all the issues raised here relate. It is to strategy and a grasp of strategic effect that one must look if there is to be a marked improvement in the American way of war.

Debate, in the form of competing ideas that reflect rival institutional interests as well as alternative strategic perspectives, has marked the history of airpower from the early 1920s to the present. It is a rare occurrence in strategic history for technology to permit exploitation of a new geographical environment. Of course, the addition of a technically dynamic third dimension to warfare could not help but fuel lively, even bitter, argument. After all, the stakes were high indeed.

It is more than 100 years since Wilbur and Orville Wright achieved the first sustained heavier-than-air flight, and those years have been liberal in providing a host of opportunities for airpower to demonstrate its contemporary prowess. Most especially, there have been conflicts great and small wherein the roles of and significance of airpower vis-à-vis landpower in particular, as well as seapower, have varied widely. Among others, Edward Luttwak has emphasized that the utility of airpower is, and has always been, highly situational.[2] This surely incontestable claim is not disputed today, at least not directly. But,

1

in politically and doctrinally guarded form, the now traditional argument over the relative importance of airpower persists.[3]

This study argues that the debate over airpower versus landpower is long past its sell-by date. The issues in this debate have by no means been foolish; indeed, they could hardly have been more serious. Similarly, there is no doubting the sincerity, though not always the objectivity, of the rival camps. Nonetheless, it is time, and then some, to call a halt to the American habit of indulging in harmful interservice combat. There are practical reasons of great complexity which account for the airpower/landpower rivalry. Those reasons, in good part pertaining to distinctive institutional cultures that express different strategic worldviews, will continue to resist efforts at reform.[4] In some respects, it is all but inconceivable for soldiers and airmen to share a common military culture. Moreover, it is probably as undesirable as it is impossible. Nevertheless, there is a frontier to competitive military and strategic attitudes and assumptions which all too easily is crossed into a region of dysfunctional disagreement. In a modest way, this study is designed to help alleviate some of the negative consequences of the continuing controversy over the relative military and strategic utility of airpower.

An important underrecognized reason why American airpower and landpower historically have had extraordinary difficulty practicing a truly joint style of warfare is the country's strategy deficit, the concept introduced to open this text. Modern America has not really "done" strategy. This deficit applies both to military strategy narrowly and to national security strategy—what the British term grand strategy—broadly.[5] It is hardly surprising that American airpower and landpower often have pursued different agendas in planning and in actual war making, given the persisting absence of a coherent strategic grip from the topmost ranks of policy.

The author is a strategic theorist, perhaps a "strategist" even, and therefore brings the bias of his trade to the subject of the airpower advantage in future warfare. However, he believes the only way forward for an American military power that is joint or integrated in practice, rather than just in name, is for the country's strategy deficit to be reduced drastically. A failure to think and behave strategically is near certain to be fatal for the proper employment of airpower, as well as for the effectiveness of US military power as an agent of high policy. But all is far from lost. As many people have argued, America needs to stop simply praising strategy, and the handful of classic texts that seek to explain its mysteries, and instead move decisively into the difficult realm of practice.

## Plan of Attack

With strategy and strategic effect as the golden threads that run through this study, as well as providing the major part of the solution to America's difficulties with war and warfare, the study opens with a direct treatment of the question, "Why this study?" The answers may surprise, and the author hopes trouble, some readers. That is followed by a brief commentary on the state of airpower theory relative to the condition of theory for the other forms of military power. To the best of the author's knowledge, no other study has noticed an important fact highlighted here: Today, mature and settled theory bearing on any of the geographically specialized forms of military power is absent. Next, the study perilously offers hostages to fortune by exposing the assumptions, issues, and arguments that drive the body of the succeeding analysis. Then, the essential and inescapable contexts of war and warfare in the future are identified and discussed. The study concludes by providing judgments on the US airpower advantage in future warfare.

A caveat is needed before moving forward. What a hypothetical Omniscient Strategic Person might identify as best strategic and military practice may not be feasible for Americans, given their general societal, strategic, and military cultures. Although this study is written by a strategic theorist, he is sufficiently experienced in the habits and attitudes prevalent in the American defense community so as not to assume that apparently superior ideas are miraculously self-effecting. People and institutions really matter.

## Why this Study?

This analysis explores the issues relevant to the advantages that should be conveyed by airpower in future warfare. However, as the opening paragraphs have established, the issue is by no means strictly military or even strategic. Surface and air forces with their distinctive cultures are in contention, as they have been for nearly 90 years. Moreover, the military cultures of the US Army and Air Force necessarily are much in debt to two other levels of culture: national strategic and, simply but pervasively, general societal. Contrary to the impression possibly conveyed by the evidence of the text thus far, the mission here is strongly positive and constructive. It is also optimistic, since strategists are not attracted to a mission impossible.

To solve a problem, one first needs to be certain that it has been diagnosed accurately. The problem, to repeat, is that the United States has a severe strategy deficit. It is, and has long been, guilty of what is known as the "tacticization" of strategy.[6] US military power does tactics well and tends to expect success at that level to translate automatically into strategic victory. Furthermore, the relatively recent advent of the computer-based information revolution has spurred speculation to the effect that the speed at which technology now functions has the consequence of eliminating the operational level of warfare. There are those who believe that information technology has shrunk distance and therefore time to a condition of near insignificance. This temporal and geographical shrinkage supposedly means that individual actions can play instantly at the strategic level with no need for operational-level purpose and direction. The operational level, the "great intellectual contribution of the continental school of strategy to 20th century military theory" as Michael Evans claims, allegedly can be discarded as obsolescent or even obsolete.[7] Tactics and strategy thus no longer need an operational-level transmission belt. This is nonsense, but it is the kind of nonsense with which we have become familiar.

The US defense community is not well endowed with practical minded strategic theorists who can do what Carl von Clausewitz specified as a necessary function. He explains that "theory exists so that one need not start afresh each time sorting out the material and plowing through it, but will find it ready to hand and in good order."[8] Strategic theory of a partial kind, which is to say that which seeks to provide order for the distinctive land, sea, air, space, cyberspace, and nuclear realms, is in anything but good order for the twenty-first century. If airpower theory is in poor condition, as many claim, it is far from lonely in that state. Lest the author's perspective and approach are misunderstood by readers who hail from the world of military action rather than military and strategic thought, he must signal endorsement of Bernard Brodie's timeless judgment on strategic theory. Brodie advised,

> Strategic thinking, or "theory," if one prefers, is nothing if not pragmatic. Strategy is a "how to do it" study, a guide to accomplishing something and doing it efficiently. As in many other branches of politics, the question that matters in strategy is: Will the idea work? More important, will it be likely to work under the special circumstances under which it will next be tested? These circumstances are not likely to be known or knowable much in advance of the moment of testing, though the uncertainty is itself a factor to be reckoned with in one's strategic doctrine.[9]

This analysis is motivated by four serious concerns.

First, much, indeed most, of the American debate about future warfare is written by people inalienably committed to a strategic view that privileges either landpower or airpower. This parochialism is rarely crude and simpleminded, but its presence can taint and skew even the best of analyses. Above all else, the committed theorist is contributing fuel to a controversy that should be dead and buried. The truth is that the more sophisticated advocates of airpower and the more balanced theorists for landpower are both correct. The relative importance of air and ground must depend upon the situation. In the future as in the past, it will vary from case to case. Of course airpower, US airpower at least, has been transformed in its tactical and, potentially, its operational effectiveness over the past 20 years, since the mid-1990s in particular.[10] The facts of the matter, as well as common sense, should indicate to those with a less parochial mindset that it is absurd to argue about which of two essential assets is in a general way the more essential. To repeat, the relative importance of airpower must vary with the strategic situation. Unfortunately, this ridiculous debate has major implications for funding, for careers, and for institutional ranking. Indeed, the author is reminded of Thucydides' famous triptych, "fear, honor, and interest," which he said comprised the principal motives behind decisions for war.[11] It would be unfair to claim that both sides of the controversy are far more interested in institutional well-being than they are in military and strategic truth. The problem is that the rival advocates of airpower primacy and of the continuation of sovereign landpower are both desperately sincere. And, it must be conceded, both are correct—given the appropriate situation. Where both are in error is in arguing their corners for a general approach to future warfare.

Second, the quality of expert strategic futurology is typically abysmal. This is not to criticize people for failing to foresee the future. Surprises happen. But it is to criticize strategic futurists, official and private, for their lack of an adequate template for strategic history. That template should be authoritative for the past, present, and the future. Naturally, there are some exceptions, but it is commonplace for high officials, civilian and military, to be guilty of the sin of *presentism.* Typically lacking any noteworthy historical education and deprived by the laws of physics of any knowledge whatsoever about the future, these officials are obliged to find their evidence about the future in present conditions. So, the future is predicted to resemble the present with only minor linear changes. The author recommends to readers' attention a comforting, but alas dangerous, advisory aphorism: "We judge the unknown to be unlikely." It is perhaps important to add the caveat that a US defense community, not known for its richness in historical understanding, is always at risk to scholarly-seeming purveyors of allegedly historically well-founded theories of change. "Power-Pointed" history can capture the imagination of those who are easily confused between Spartans and Athenians.

Third, technological innovation lies at the heart of the argument for the privileging of airpower in a new American way in warfare. There is nothing wrong with that, as far as it goes. Unfortunately for the integrity of the argument, technology is only one of warfare's seven contexts. To assess intelligently the strategic and political implications of new technology, one must command a comprehensive theory of war and warfare. This is not just a matter of speculation about the future. It so happens that we are blessed with variably reliable access to no fewer than 2,500 years of strategic history. The twenty-first century is not exactly the first period in the human adventure when science and technology have shifted, or threatened to shift, the balance among military instruments. If we choose to be ignorant of what history can teach us, the choice and cost are ours. The great Prussian theorist had this to say about the third reason for this study, "But in war more than in any other subject we must begin by looking at the nature of the whole; for here more than elsewhere the part and the whole must always be thought of together."[12]

In other words, for the purposes of this study it has to be unsound to develop theories of landpower and airpower, among others, unless they are firmly grasped by an overarching theory of war and warfare. Plainly, a holistic theory of warfare is lacking today. As a direct consequence, argument about the strategic implications of airpower's recent transformation or the allegedly enduring necessity for the presence of "*the man* [our man, naturally; CSG] *on the scene with the gun*" is conducted out of context and even, one can assert, out of paradigm.[13] In the latter regard, if a holistic view of war and warfare is absent, there can be no dominant paradigm worthy of the ascription. Of course there will be rival paradigms which express the deepest beliefs of true disciples of one or another of the partial theories of warfare: for example, victory through decisive land battle or victory through airpower.

Fourth and finally, this study is designed and executed to contribute to the reduction of America's long-standing strategy deficit. In the United States, strategy is neither well understood nor, as an inevitable consequence, well conceived—when it is conceived at all—and executed. This author does not know how to approach the roles and relative influence of airpower in future warfare except in strategic perspective. This perspective requires appreciation of the central significance of the concept, and prospective reality, of strategic effect. As the author has explained elsewhere, strategy is the bridge that should link the realm of policy with the world of its instruments, in the case of this study with policy's military agency.[14] The defining characteristic of strategy, and the quality strategic, is instrumentality. It is the task of strategy to translate the ends of policy into the ways and means for their achievement. In practice, the process of strategy making and adjustment entails a dialogue between policy makers and soldiers as aspiration, theory, and plans meet the reality of a sentient and reacting enemy.[15] It so happens that strategy is an exceptionally challenging function to perform competently. We are blessed with many more expert politicians and soldiers than strategists. The job of the strategist may be likened to currency conversion when there is no stable exchange rate. For the desired, at least for an acceptable, political outcome, the threat or actual use of military power has to be converted into strategic effect upon the overall course of a conflict. This is no mean feat. History records unambiguously that despite the prodigious military accomplishments of the past century, the United States has rarely performed with a strategic skill worthy of its combat forces. More to the point, the way forward in advancing understanding of the benefits and limitations of America's airpower advantage has to be through a considerable improvement in the quality of the country's strategy.

## Airpower Theory

Scholars disagree, as scholars will, over the issue of whether the history of airpower reveals the leadership of ideas and doctrine over technology or vice versa. Both points of view are defensible, though this study leans toward the former. The issue is important because it bears upon the future of the airpower advantage. It has generated rival interpretations of airpower history: either technology has been chasing ideas on use or ideas and doctrine have been rationalizing what technology provided largely uninvited. Each school of opinion advances a distinctive view of the preferred path forward. The technology ascendant school looks to theory to provide airpower with its allegedly missing conceptual framework. The doctrine first school, in contrast, emphasizes the need to build airpower capable of delivering the effects required by powerful ideas. This study suggests that neither approach is helpful when employed preclusively. It argues that to develop airpower for its maximum advantage, the focus must first be expanded to encompass the whole of a conflict. The airpower story, or however else one elects to phrase it, should be conceived, designed, and executed only in the context of war and warfare as a whole. There should be no need to stress the point that the identical rule applies to landpower, seapower, spacepower, and cyberpower. Airpower is not being singularized. Given the extent of the assertions in this paragraph, it is useful to quote a few especially potent examples of the rival perspectives on the significance of ideas in airpower history.

8

Probably the most quoted claim for technological leadership is that of David MacIsaac.

> Air power, the generic term widely adopted to identify this phenomenon [advent of manned aircraft], has nonetheless yet to find a clearly defined or unchallenged place in the history of military or strategic theory. There has been no lack of theorists, but they have had only limited influence in a field where the effects of technology and the deeds of practitioners have from the beginning played greater roles than have ideas.[16]

To drive home his claim for technological ascendancy, MacIsaac concludes his analysis with this clever thought, "One might conclude, with some distress, that technology itself may be today's primary air power theorist: that invention may, for the moment be the mother of application."[17] It sounds plausible, but is it true? In support of MacIsaac's position one can quote the opinion of that greatly respected airpower historian, I.B. Holley. "The airplane has been around for nearly one hundred years, but, given its remarkable potential, surely one is surprised by the dearth of really comprehensive thinkers and theorists on airpower."[18]

However, the "technology rules" school does not reign unchallenged. In the best, which is to say analytically the most balanced and penetrating book offering a general theory of war and of strategy written in the twentieth century, Adm J.C. Wylie, USN, argued as follows:

> The air theory, now so prominent in the minds of all of the world [1967; CSG], is unique in that it was born as an idea rather than developed from experience.

> [T]he air theory is unique in the sense that it exists primarily as theory rather than as a system of tested experiments that have grown gradually into a meaningful pattern over the years.[19]

The final quotation illustrating the rival arguments, or assertions perhaps, is a contemporary judgment offered by historian and defense analyst, Frederick W. Kagan.

> This dismissal of the role of theory [by military professionals; CSG] has never been valid—theories of war have driven the planning and conduct of military operations since the mid-eighteenth century at least—but it is nowhere less valid than in the consideration of air power. From the first time a man put a bomb on a plane to drop on the enemy [1911; CSG], the planning and conduct of air operations has been a thoroughly theoretical undertaking.[20]

The debate inevitably is inconclusive, though it is probably true to claim that most of airpower's critics are persuaded that technology has led ideas. On balance, as noted already, the author is not at all convinced that ideas typically have followed in technology's wake. However, there is no denying the ease with which both points of view can find historical counter-examples to score debating points. The clearest and most dramatic example of science and technology leaving strategic ideas far behind was, of course, the atomic bomb. The Allied military establishments did not request nuclear weapons, in fact did not even know that they could be built, and certainly were undecided for many years over their strategic meaning. They were not alone in their confusion. Policy makers and most defense theorists were similarly confounded, at least for the better part of a decade.

As a belated caveat, it is necessary to remember that this study focuses on US airpower and on the kinds of warfare for which the United States needs to prepare in the future. Often, American defense theorists and commentators forget that the problems and possible solutions that consume their attention are, in major part, unique to the current global superpower. Size does matter. While there are vital general truths about war, warfare, peace, order, and strategy, once one descends into the zone of real-world application, one is faced with challenges of a scope and kind that no other security community must meet. Writing as an Anglo-American strategic theorist, it is easy to neglect to notice, for example, that one theory of seapower does not fit all cases adequately. Both of the leading theorists of seapower, Alfred Thayer Mahan (American) and Sir Julian Corbett (British) wrote for a dominant navy. But few countries have aspired to maritime dominance. Today, most countries' navies more closely resemble the US Coast Guard in missions and capabilities than they do the US Navy. Naturally one can theorize for airpower, landpower, spacepower, and now cyberpower. But while assuredly there are bodies of general wisdom governing both warfare as a whole and combat in each distinctive environment, the contexts for each country's airpower (and the other forms of military power) are unique and so must be application of the general theory.

The extended US defense community, certainly in its official and industrial ranks, by and large is organized to provide and support the individual services. As a consequence, there is a widespread lack of appreciation of the scope of the problem that drives this study. Specifically, it seeks to understand and advance America's airpower advantage in future warfare. It may have escaped the notice of many defense analysts and commentators, but every major element of, or geographical dimension to, US military power is facing deep uncertainty over its roles and relative significance. The study is primarily about airpower, but its argument, analysis, and conclusions cannot be thus narrowly restricted. In summary form, the strategic condition of America's geographically specific military power, plus the nuclear element, is as follow.

1. *Landpower* knows that it must be dominant in irregular warfare, but it is under increasing challenge from airpower in regular combat. Since a regular style of warfare is the US Army's far preferred modus operandi, this menace from altitude has some unwelcome implications for favored, very expensive high-technology transformation plans. Is landpower theory, with its devotion to operational art, essentially obsolete now that non Army-organic airpower can maul, and perhaps defeat, enemy regular forces in the deep battle?[21]

2. *Seapower* is not threatened so directly by the recent evolution of, or revolution in, US airpower, but it is vulnerable to the charge that it plans to retain a blue-water focus, even though future combat is expected to be confined to green or even brown water. Tomorrow's enemies may not contest US control on the high seas, but rather seek to deny access to Eurasian geography. Does the US Navy feel confident that it comprehends its roles and its necessary capabilities in future warfare? The author thinks not.

3. *Spacepower* has evolved, system by system, to answer particular needs. Quite literally, there is no theory of spacepower worthy of the title. Is Benjamin S. Lambeth correct when he anticipates a functional, effective merger of airpower and spacepower, despite the contrasting geophysics of the atmosphere and space?[22] Or, are the "space cadets" thinking soundly when they argue that for space

to be approached prudently as a future environment for warfare (on historical precedent an inevitable development) its military needs should be in the hands of a space-dedicated organization? At present, the geophysical vacuum is well matched by the vacuum in theory, concepts, ideas, and plausible forward-looking doctrine.

4.  *Cyberpower* is in an even greater state of incoherence than is spacepower. This is scarcely surprising given its novelty. Nonetheless, in common with spacepower, it is here to stay and it needs to be accommodated in the American way in warfare. As threat and as opportunity, cyberpower is a challenge to all the levels of warfare. For the time being, it is open season for speculative theory on the relative significance of the computer. In addition, the doors are wide open to scientific and technological prediction as to the pace, direction, and military utility of electronic innovation. To say that strategic theory for cyberpower currently is still in its infancy would be a gross understatement.

5.  *Nuclear weapons* triggered the invention of the theory of stable mutual deterrence, the centerpiece of US nuclear thinking for 35 years. Today that theory is almost wholly irrelevant to contemporary and anticipated future political and military-strategic contexts. In addition, serious doubts have been raised about the historical validity of the theory.[23] Since the collapse of the Union of Soviet Socialist Republics (USSR), credible evidence, from Soviet general staff sources in particular, suggests strongly that American assumptions about Soviet nuclear thinking and war planning were seriously in error.[24] Be that as it may, the point is that today the United States is rewriting its nuclear strategy for coherence and complementarity with the new competence of precision conventional strike, and is seeking to "tailor" deterrence to the character of specific foes. At this time, US nuclear strategy is being debated energetically in the aftermath of the root-and-branch Nuclear Policy Review (NPR) of 2002.[25] Some of the most cherished beliefs of American arms controllers about stable deterrence have been shown to have rested on wishful thinking. For more than 40 years, the orthodox American view held that there was only a single

nuclear doctrinal enlightenment; that American theorists were the first to grasp the essentials of that enlightenment; and that, with the aid of some American education on the matter, Soviet officials either had, or soon would, come to share the dominant American view.

It should be clear enough from this brief review and analysis that literally every major element in US military power currently faces an uncertain future. Two of those elements, spacepower and cyberpower, are completely lacking in theoretical, even just conceptual, support while landpower, seapower, and nuclear weapons are all menaced by changing political, military-strategic, and technological contexts.[26] These facts should ease some of the anxieties of air-minded persons. Everyone and everything are having difficulty understanding where their kind of military power fits, how that fit will vary according to the character of specific conflicts, and how significant their roles will be in relation to the other players in the supposedly joint team. It is noticeable that in typical stovepipe fashion, the separate US military communities are earnestly and, in many ways properly, worrying more about their particular roles in future warfare than they are about the overall conduct of that warfare.

If airpower is short of conceptual support, which this study begs leave to doubt, the answer does, or would, not lie in the creation of some master air theory. Instead, suitable ideas for the roles of airpower in future warfare can be developed only in the context of a whole theory of warfare. Environmentally privileged theory for landpower, seapower, airpower, and the rest can only promote interservice antagonism at the expense of comprehension of the whole challenge of warfare. The best that a cluster of geographically specific theories can achieve is a minimum consensus, not a truly joint, let alone integrated, approach to deterrence and actual combat.

## Issues and Arguments

Airpower can be decisive in both warfare and in war. Note the qualification "can." Also, airpower may not be decisive. It may just be a supporting agent for a struggle on land. This reads like a typical piece of scholarly equivocation, of an academic trying to have it both ways, avoiding a commitment. Such an impression would be wrong. It is the case that airpower can influence a conflict, or a potential conflict via deterrence and coercion generally, on a wide spectrum of possibilities. That is the way it has been historically, it is today, and one must assume it will be tomorrow. One restricted size in airpower's strategic utility, great or small, emphatically does not fit its future tasks and responsibilities in the US arsenal.

At this juncture in the study, having cleared some dead wood and set the scene, the author assembles a summary of the arguments and issues which carry the work forward and through to its conclusions. Most of these vital items have been raised already in passing, but it is necessary to collect them to present the clearest possible picture of the main thrusts of the argument.

*The United States needs a reasonably authoritative theory of war and warfare which accommodates a theory of airpower.* That theory of airpower, currently absent along with the master theory into which it must fit, is not, cannot be and must not substitute for, a theory of war and warfare. It may be necessary to clarify a definitional point. Warfare refers to the actual waging of war, pre-eminently though not exclusively to fighting. In contrast, war is a total relationship of belligerency that naturally includes warfare. Not all of airpower's true disciples, by which is meant people who argue largely from faith and are not moveable by evidence, have distinguished between war and warfare. They have conveniently conflated the two.[27] For a classic example, Air Chief Marshal Sir Arthur Harris, then the commander of the Royal Air Force's Bomber Command, claimed as follows: "We can wreck Berlin from end to end if the USAAF [United States Army Air Forces] will come in on it. It will cost between us 400-500 aircraft. It will cost Germany the war."[28] Similar beliefs were expressed over the wars in Korea, Vietnam, Gulf War I, Kosovo 1999, Afghanistan in 2001 for a while at least, and Gulf War II, again only for a while.

*Future warfare will assume many forms.* It will not neatly nest in a binary way into regular or irregular categories. Some conflicts will embrace both, probably simultaneously.[29] This less than startling safe prediction means that the future airpower advantage in its many forms, all contributing to the key quality, strategic effect, will be diverse in delivery and importance. It is not a simple strategic tale to attempt to predict in detail, assess, and debate with skeptics.

Next, for the airpower advantage to secure strategic results of value, it must serve a national policy and a grand and overall military strategy that are feasible, coherent, and politically sensible. If these basic requirements are not met, airpower, no matter how impeccably applied tactically and operationally, will be employed as a waste of life, taxes, and, frankly, trust between the sharp end of America's spear and its shaft. This situation is by no means unlikely in the future, if history, including current events, is a guide.

*The strategic advantage that airpower can convey depends entirely upon the contexts of war, crisis, and peace.* These contexts (the author chooses to identify seven) determine, yes determine (the word that scholars fear to use), what the war is about, how it is waged, and indeed everything about the conflict. The seven contexts comprise the following:[30]

- Political

- Social-cultural

- Economic

- Technological

- Military-Strategic

- Geographical

- Historical

These are sufficiently broad, yet also adequately focused, to capture all that we need to know about the conditions that govern the terms on which a conflict, in time of peace or actual war, must be waged. As many theorists have argued, correctly in the view of this study, airpower is highly situational in its ability to deliver advantage. And that idea of situational airpower is just another way of saying that the airpower advantage is strongly contextual.

It should be to the amazement of none to read now that *airpower itself needs a coherent strategy of employment, and by no means only of "kinetic" employment* as the currently fashionable euphemism has it. Future warfare must, and will, be joint and perhaps even integrated in well "internetted" character. This is not quite the radical innovation, let alone discovery as a desideratum, that some people believe. Although US airpower has a distinctly checkered history of cooperation with landpower and seapower, in practice it has always been obliged to function to a degree jointly. There are important historical examples of superb cooperation for joint effectiveness. One can cite US airpower supporting, literally enabling, Gen Douglas MacArthur's painful climb from New Guinea up the Japanese-occupied Dutch East Indies towards Java. Or, one could mention Maj Gen Elwood R. "Pete" Quesada's somewhat disobedient and officially strongly disliked insistence upon placing his mighty tactical airpower assets in direct support of ground forces. Quesada, who commanded the USAAF's IX Fighter Command of the Ninth Air Force, provided such support despite formidable service opposition, including that from the chief, Gen Henry H. "Hap" [for "Happy"; CSG] Arnold. Quesada's 1,600 P-47 Thunderbolt fighter bombers, which were superb aircraft for close air support and tactical interdiction for isolation of the battlefield, made an immeasurably great contribution to the hugely risky operation that was D-day.[31] For much more recent examples of excellent cooperation between airpower and landpower, one must mention the conventional campaign against the Taliban in Afghanistan in 2001 and again the conventional, regular "march up country" campaign to seize Baghdad, almost by a surprise *coup de main*, in 2003.[32] Those brilliantly successful brief campaigns did not end the warfare, alas, but they undoubtedly showcased what airpower could do when it adopted a coherent and appropriate strategy.

*The potential value of airpower in future warfare is a spectrum of possibilities, depending upon the contexts or situation.* It is not an *either/or* quality and quantity of strategic utility. Unless this elementary claim is recognized and fully understood, there is little prospect of the true value of airpower being properly assessed as to its strategic effect or potential.

*Next, one should not assume that complete air domination is America's as by divine, or would-be hegemonic, right.* Most airpersons, especially those at the sharp end, know this, but many people who should know better are apt to forget that warfare is by its very nature a competitive project. Recall that in the war-

16

fare against Serbia in 1999, allied, largely US, aircraft were ordered to fly no lower than 15,000 feet to eliminate or significantly reduce the dangers from ground fire. In the future, America's anticipated airpower advantage could well be eroded by an intelligent enemy. One who may be able to render the skies less benign than American landpower has long come to expect. Not only will some foes be able to menace US airpower directly and kinetically, but they will be powerfully motivated to reduce that airpower's effectiveness through assaults upon US spacepower. Those attacks would probably aim to degrade global positioning system signals in particular. Also, well planned cyberattacks against America's heavily internetted forces are so predictable as to warrant labeling as a certainty.[33] US airpower could well, and should assume that it will, have to perform in hazardous military contexts in some kinds of future warfare.

*American airpower is a very great asymmetrical advantage.* At least, it is very great if it is properly equipped, trained, provided with suitable concepts of operation—doctrine—and properly employed within a coherent strategy in the service of a prudent overall strategy and national policy. US enemies in the future are fairly certain to enjoy some major asymmetrical advantages (e.g., the initiative, knowledge of the terrain, and relative strength of political motivation). Airpower intelligently prepared and employed can and should go a long way toward leveling a battlespace in contexts that otherwise would see friendly forces possibly fatally disadvantaged. America should seek to squeeze every possible gain from its predictable asymmetrical domination of the skies, even as the quality of that domination increasingly is challenged as it certainly will be.

*It is not possible to predict with total confidence the character of future warfare.* Admiral Wylie, quoted earlier, offers these wise words:

> We cannot predict with certainty the pattern of the war for which we prepare ourselves. We cannot, with reasonable certainty, forecast the time, the place, the scope, the intensity, the course of a war. I think no man ever has. A strategy for an entire war is not predictable (emphasis in original).[34]

Two pages later, the Admiral sums up his message thus, "But planning for certitude is the greatest of all military mistakes, as military history demonstrates all too vividly."[35] America be warned. The US military establishment is in danger of enjoying an overconfidence based imprudently upon favorable order-of-battle comparisons. Time and again, devastating surprise has been achieved not by the sudden appearance of some novel items of equipment, but rather in the unexpected ways in which familiar military assets are used. Given the deep contemporary uncertainty about the effectiveness of space and cyber warfare for two leading examples, it is not difficult to understand how fragile must be official predictions on the character of future warfare.

*For reasons that are both pragmatically sensible as well as deeply cultural, one can expect airpower to remain the most favored military agency in the American way of warfare.*[36] Sometimes this popular, and therefore political, appeal will not be well judged. It must depend upon the particular contexts. Understanding of the inherent strengths and limitations of airpower, as well as of the exact meaning of airpower (the range and scope of its diverse components), is not exactly widespread. To most Americans, airpower equals dropping explosives on "bad guys"—well, mostly bad guys. Such activities as logistic support; medevac; intelligence, surveillance, and reconnaissance (ISR); and search and rescue, for a few examples, have a low profile among armchair amateur warriors. Because airpower holds a treasured place in the affections of an unmilitary, yet rather warlike, American public, there is a constant danger that much more will be asked and expected of it than it can deliver. Since America's now longstanding love affair with airpower is significantly cultural, it is futile to hope for a transformation, to resort to a familiar concept, in that affection to a condition better suited to the varying situations of conflict. Airpower is the epitome of high technology, high technology is America, and Americans expect to wage high-technology warfare, successfully of course.

*One should not take a narrowly focused view of the advantages of airpower by concentrating strictly on the variable conditions of actual warfare.* Airpower has amply demonstrated its strategic effectiveness, as well as its limitations, in contexts of watchful and tense peace, for deterrence, to police some of the conditions of adversary behavior that are legally and therefore politically prohibited, and for coercion or even some reassurance—deliberately visible operational arms control, for example—in times of incipient or actual crisis.

*It is important for those sincerely convinced of the great advantages conferred by superior airpower not to understate its systemic and situational limitations.* There is nothing to be gained by silence or exaggerated denial on this topic from the ranks of airpersons. The US defense community is well populated by strong critics of airpower who will be only too pleased to exploit that silence and exaggeration to show how untrustworthy is the airpower story as delivered by its truest disciples. Error has a way of being punished. The moral has biblical authority. The advantages conferred by airpower must vary with the contexts of its employment.

*The balance of relative influence upon the course of regular conventional war has been shifting for 20 years or more in favor of airpower as compared to landpower.* This is and should be undeniable. Needless to say, this plain tactical and operational fact is flatly denied by landpower theorists and executors who hold to the fundamental belief that victory can only ultimately be achieved by the decisive engagement of armies. The landpower stance and doctrine are not all wrong. It depends upon the situation. The claim for America achieving a transformation in the tactical, operational, and therefore, logically, the strategic and political effectiveness of its airpower became ever more plausible as the 1990s advanced. However, Kosovo struck a sour note in that, although airpower succeeded in the absence of a NATO landpower intervention, the coercive air campaign lasted an embarrassing 78 days rather than the confidently anticipated three.[37] Moving on, so effective and innovative was the joint-to-integrated use of airpower in Afghanistan (against a Taliban that unwisely chose to stand and stage a regular resistance) that there was much contemporary speculation claiming that a "new American way of war" had just been discovered and practiced to a brilliant outcome.[38] Strategic history has a habit of laughing at premature optimists. The reality and relevance of the shift that privileges airpower over landpower are highly context dependent. And even in situations where airpower unquestionably is the force that decides who wins, usually there will still be vital missions that only landpower can undertake. The controversy over airpower versus landpower for relative influence is alive and all too well at present and, sadly, predictably far into the future.

The general thrust of this analysis is to identify the advantages that should be conveyed by leadership in the air (and in space and cyberspace). Therefore, it is only prudent to take notice of some of the more perilous of the factors that can, not necessarily will, let alone must, limit airpower's relative effectiveness. Consider these potential factors that would weaken the airpower contribution to war fighting.

1. Poor air strategy, operational artistry, or tactics.

2. Inappropriate air assets.

3. Loss or serious degradation of support from space systems.

4. Serious damage through effective cyberattacks.

5. Incompetent or inappropriate mixes and uses of land-power and seapower; meaning that the prospects for success in the war on land or at sea are beyond rescue by US land-based airpower.

6. Finally, for the killer limitation, US national security policy and possibly its national security strategy, as well as its overall national military strategy, may all be so dysfunctional that they cannot be rescued from defeat by a dominant airpower, no matter how that airpower is employed.

And now it is necessary to turn to speculative, and it must be admitted controversial, consideration of the contexts of future warfare.

## Future Warfare: Contextual Realities

Nothing in this study is, or could be, more important than the contexts of future warfare. They cannot determine exactly which events will occur or which decisions will be taken, but they will provide just about everything else. To explain, the seven chosen contexts (see above) provide the political situation which generates war and therefore warfare, foreign and domestic; the social-cultural ideologies, attitudes, habits of mind, and behavior patterns that to a degree program different security communities and organizations within those communities in their approach to issues of war and peace;[39] the economic wherewithal to raise and sustain armed forces; the technological terms upon which warfare is threatened and waged; the military-strategic relationship between antagonists, as well as details of the actual contemporary military "grammar" of war (to borrow from Clausewitz);[40] the geographical setting for hostilities, be it global or localized; and the historical placement of war and warlike happenings since all wars have origins and consequences in the stream of time.

Could we only be certain in our speculation, understanding of these contexts should enable us to achieve near perfection in strategy were it not for four major sources of difficulty. These are (1) the active intervention of enemies to spoil our unilateral picture of the future; (2) the inability of our institutions of government, civilian and military, to deliver an approximation to perfection substantially through bureaucratic, which is to say political, endeavor in the matching of ways, means, and policy ends; (3) the unpredictability of human behavior, as our future political leaders sometimes will make choices that do not appear to correspond to the familiar rules of rational choice; and (4) the certain non-linearities of accident and surprise. This contextual framework, by theatrical analogy, should capture everything about the play that will be future warfare, save only for the particular interconnected choices made by competing statespeople who have some discretion as to how they can play their parts. In this section, the study will go far beyond the bare framework of contextuality and venture heavily and contentiously into prediction. Some readers may find more value in the contextual approach adopted than in the judgments of the strategist-author.

**Political Context**

Since war is always about politics, the political context must be the source for all future warfare of every character. If the primary motive of organized violence is criminal profit, culturally induced and licensed recreation, or just sheer hooliganism on a large scale, it cannot be warfare. However, those blights sometimes merge into, certainly are inadvertently promoted by, wartime conditions.

How will future political contexts, domestic and foreign, impact upon the prospects for warfare? History obliges us to re-

21

spect as a fact that its strategic dimension has been constant, albeit not constantly active on the largest of scales.[41] The prospects for the twenty-first century could be much worse than they seem at present, but these are very early years and there is ample cause for concern already.

The good news is that unlike the twentieth century from 1917 until 1991, the ideological rivalries that contributed so powerfully to interstate rivalry, ambition, and anxiety are all but defunct, save only in two respects whose influence is easy to exaggerate. On the hostile side, the global jihad proclaimed by al Qaeda in 1998 assuredly is a source of contemporary and future warfare. But, unless its decidedly irregular and unofficial behaviors can promote interstate warfare, the challenge it can pose must be minor compared with the greatest of threats registered and over-come over the course of the past 100 years. Even an al Qaeda affiliate with a "dirty" radiological device or two will not compare with the perils posed during the Cold War. The other major ideo-logical element alive in global politics is, and for cultural rea-sons to a degree must remain, America's enduring commitment to spread liberal democracy and the free market.

A major political and strategic rivalry between, perhaps among, the United States, China, and the Russian Federation is unavoidable and confidently predictable. None of the three wants war, but Thucydides' "fear, honor, and interest" mandate the near certainty that their conflicting interests will result in a new political architecture of antagonistic alignments. The United States will strive to remain the sole global superpower; the state that counts for the most on nearly every question of global security. This American stance has become habitual, it is the product of the reality of resources and superior wealth, and it is the existing situation.

Both China and Russia are strongly motivated to reduce the American role of global judge, jury, and sheriff. Neither wishes to risk war with Washington, but the century has barely begun. Global security politics were not unduly ominous from the per-spective of 1907, at least to contemporary optimists. And we are not short of such people today.

China does not accept the extant measure of US global influ-ence. Why? Because it fears America's ability to harm its in-creasingly global range of interests, and hence by extension its domestic political stability; it is acutely sensitive to the dishonor of being obliged to tolerate American leadership and unilateralism; and it fears that America's undoubted strength could overmatch China and frustrate her drive for primacy.

As for the new-old Russia, the contextual reality of the twenty-first century is that this country has serious irredentist claims in all directions save the north, and even the Arctic will return to its erstwhile somewhat contested state as a result of global warming. Russia is ruled by a former KGB functionary of modest ability. His chosen political partners and most likely successors should be assumed to be people of similar attitude, if not background. Russia is an increasingly loose cannon on a notably rolling international security deck.

Both China and Russia are potentially unstable in their domestic politics and will be compelled by the authoritative logic of the balance of power to seek friends and allies if they are to discipline an unacceptable US hegemony. India, Japan, Brazil, and EU-Europe will remain second or third-order players of international security politics, while the Middle East will continue to fester from its multiple troubles. That festering could well occasion a regional nuclear conflict. Elsewhere, warfare will remain as endemic as it has always been.[42]

### Socio-Cultural Context

Liberal optimists who believe that future warfare will be much reduced by the spread of benign globally recognized and practiced norms are certain to be disappointed. Most people in most places throughout history have not favored warfare. It did not make much difference. World War II was not a popular war, in prospect not even in Germany. It does not take much for pacific norms, conventions, laws, and international institutions to count for nought. All it takes is one country, even one person in the wrong country, to be strongly risk-accepting, highly ambitious, and well enough endowed with material assets and a sufficiency of local political support for the history of a decade, or a century, to be changed much for the worse.

The attractive conceits we humans have learnt (or are learning), the benefits of peace, are increasingly interdependent through the wonders of globalization; and suchlike claims are by no means false. However, unfortunately, those arguments have been made repeatedly since the conclusion of the first of the cycle of modern great wars in 1815. And one should never forget that there is not a truly global culture for a no less truly global society or community.[43] If such is advancing today, which may be the case, it is doing so at so deliberate a pace, and in such prospectively hostile conditions, that it can serve as no sort of a guide to the future of warfare for any period of interest to this study.

**Economic Context**

Economic motivations for war would appear to make little sense in an intricately globalized world. Does not Chinese industry require American and European consumers? Russians and Iranians cannot drink their oil and gas, and so forth. Alas, the economic story of the twenty-first century is not entirely a prospectively happy one. There are many (over)confident predictions by mainly American techno-optimists. But, there will be a growing energy shortage for a sharply increasing world population whose well being must be menaced in the very areas most at risk to adverse climate change. The extent and severity of the coming crisis are deeply uncertain, but the fact of the trend and its inescapable outcomes are not. Those outcomes will include increasing competition for the staples of life, competition for productive land, and, of course, mass migration.

Additionally, the theory that a rising tide of globalized prosperity raises all boats is both not true enough and encourages an unsound conclusion. Globalization, it is now generally recognized, raises some boats almost precipitately while others are left rotting on the mud-flats of the world economy. More to the international security point, while the genuine losers in the information technology (IT) enabled global economy will be able to suffer and promote only a very local mayhem, some of the major winners will want to win more, more rapidly. They will be prepared to give economic history a helping push by challenging the still-Western (i.e., US) authored international rules and institutional frameworks that govern world trade and finance.

24

## Technological Context

Extensive past experience demonstrates that technological prediction is close to worthless.[44] Great unexpected discoveries are exactly that, unexpected. Typically, they are made by individuals or small teams, not by massively funded official or industrial programs. Often they are the thoroughly serendipitous product of a single brain. There is a concept that covers the case; it is genius. Current technological trends are easy to identify, but they offer no reliable guide to the future because they rest upon a basis in science, which is to say in scientific discovery, that cannot be predicted, even by scientists themselves.

To predict the technological future for warfare many decades into the future is a perilous undertaking. However, we cannot simply throw up our hands in despair. Fortunately, there is some limited help at hand. First, given the lead-time for science to turn into usable military technology and given the porous nature of the barriers protecting national secrets in an all but universally digitized world, advance notice of foreign technology is generally attainable. Much less attainable is understanding of just what new technologies will mean for alien strategic and military cultures and their possibly cunning plans. Since those cultures are likely themselves to be in doubt as to how new capabilities can best be exploited, US uncertainty will be thoroughly understandable.

One can be certain that America's principal foreign challengers in this century, who must be China and Russia, just possibly in combination, will seek asymmetric advantage in order to degrade the potency of America's military, political, and economic strengths.[45] Already, the Chinese are working hard to achieve a useful, and prospectively an actually disabling, space denial capability.[46] In addition, China is devoting major efforts to modernize its armed forces for combat in information-led battlespace by developing a credible access denial capability resting upon a large force of both nuclear and conventional missiles, ballistic and cruise. However, precise guidance at longer ranges will remain a severe challenge for many years to come.

The Russians have decided that the centerpiece of their return to the higher table of states that matter, aside from a coercive energy policy, is a sophisticated, modernizing, nuclear missile arsenal.[47] This arsenal is matched by a doctrine of very early nuclear use and by full appreciation of the disabling damage that nuclear weapon effects (electromagnetic pulse most especially) could have upon an enemy dependent upon an intimately network-centric style of military operations. The USSR was obliged to file for reorganization, but Russia remains strong in basic science and it has a gigantic nuclear infrastructure that continues to function well enough to be able to innovate impressively.

## Military-Strategic Context

The military-strategic context of the twenty-first century cannot continue to be as favorable to the United States as it is at present. China, Russia, India, Japan, and even EU-Europe either are or could become global science-based technological superstates. That condition, in a world beset by life-and-death resource shortages and the continuing authority of the all too familiar triad of "fear, honor, and interest," means that in some national cases elementary prudence and a measure of ambition will translate wealth and technology into military power.

America is currently Number One in regular military capability in every geographical environment. This is historically unprecedented. In the sole possible comparison, even the Romans never dominated Persia or the Germanic tribes beyond the Rhine and the Danube for long, or simultaneously. From the topmost rung, America's relative military, and hence strategic and political, standing can only move in one direction. Competitors will learn from the successes and failures of the military leader, and will invest selectively in the most cost effective answers to America's strengths. Future foes will make strategic and military choices based not only on what Americans would judge to be rational cost-benefit choices but also their behavior will bear local cultural stamps.

The continuing military transformation drive of the US armed forces is in large degree culturally mandated by the technology momentum of the IT revolution. But all too often, it has been propelled by unconvincing strategic rationales. In large measure, this absence of plausible strategic logic has been the product of the threat vacuum in which America happily and unexpectedly found itself in the inter-war decade of the 1990s. Between Christmas 1991 and 9/11, the US threat board was

bereft of any really serious menace. Since warfare is by definition a competitive endeavor, this vacuum made the task of
American defense planners exceptionally difficult. Money for
the military is tight in a democracy when the voting public is
not frightened. And even in the expert depths of the extended
defense community, predictions of future warfare were not sufficiently convincing to provide useful guidance. Those few
among us who anticipated a hostile China and Russia were
generally dismissed as locked in an archaic worldview. Today
our anticipations have turned into predictions. They are in competition not so much with the view that major interstate war has
passed into history, but rather with the extremely popular post
9/11 assumption, one can hardly say argument, that future warfare for Americans will be almost entirely irregular in character.
After all, is not that the reality of the 2000s?

It is the view of this study that the United States will need to
develop and sustain armed forces adaptable to warfare all along
its bloody spectrum. From the occasional terrorist outrage to
large-scale nuclear conflict, a global superpower is obliged by
its values and its continuing immense strengths to play police-
man for international order. It must do so both on its own be-
half and for the general good.[48] Americans would soon find a
policy doctrine of non-intervention to be thoroughly unsustainable,
notwithstanding its obvious popular attraction. The trouble is that
America's assets, though large, are not infinite. Also, America's
policy makers will not be reliably wise or competent while its official
strategists, should it have one or two at the time, will need to
exercise choice over the ways and means to effect the ends
desired by politics. If warfare of all kinds certainly lies before
Americans in this century, what should be US military strategy?
Where should the balance be struck among capabilities to ex-
cel in regular and irregular warfare, and how fungible is the
military power generated primarily for each of these unduly
neat *conceptual* categories?

The primary source of the confidence with which this study
anticipates an unhappily active and highly varied future in the
American waging of warfare can only be historical. One should
be impressed by the master narrative of 2,500 years which has
been dominated by its strategic, which is to say its force-related,
theme. This time, in the twenty-first century, history might be

27

radically different. That could be true, but it is so improbable that no responsible US government or strategic advisor could offer it as an actionable anticipation, let alone as prediction.

### Geographical Context

What will be the geographical contexts for future warfare? Where will Americans have to fight and for what goals? Will the warfare serve unlimited or limited ends? These are not idle rhetorical questions. They bear directly upon the scope and scale of strategic and military challenges and, as a consequence, upon the balance among geographically specialized armed forces. Geography still matters greatly. Admittedly, it matters less than it did before airpower could function reliably and effectively in bad weather, a very recent improvement, but it does still matter. Future warfare will include action in and through no fewer than five environments: land, sea, air, space, and cyberspace.

We are advised, with some good reasons, that America should concentrate on commanding "the commons." By this, Barry Posen extends Mahan's powerful concept to include the commons of the air, space, and cyberspace.[49] Minimize the placing of American boots on culturally alien ground, let us control everything else. Posen's analysis and suggestion are persuasive but, alas, fundamentally unsound. Today, one cannot know with "rock-like confidence" exactly where, why, and how the United States will wish to fight in the future.[50] But what is known with the confidence born of extensive experience is that every war requires the waging of warfare in a manner somewhat unique to its circumstances. In particular, the airpower contribution will be different in detail from case to case. Fortunately, there is much about airpower, as indeed about war and warfare in general, that is common to many or even all cases. Still, the objective facts of physical and social-cultural geography do not by any means present a standard battlespace. It is noticeable how in the on-going debate over the relative future importance of landpower and airpower, rival debaters are obliged to select an environmental context that flatters the strengths and discounts the limitations of their case.

As a challenging thought to some readers, the author suggests that for most military technologies (considered singly but more intelligently, especially, in combination), there is an equivalent to Clausewitz's concept of "the culminating point of victory."[51] In partial translation, Clausewitz points to a diminishing, and eventually a strongly negative, rate of return to effort when behavior or capability is permitted a dominant role beyond its competence. Also, there is always an enemy out there, determined to reduce the military and strategic value of America's more or less jointly fighting, semi-transformed forces. Transformation is an essentially endless process, systemically conducted with high risks of activating potent regrets downstream. The author suggests that the transformation of US airpower, a process about which Benjamin Lambeth has written brilliantly, is approaching the edge of its envelope of war-fighting effectiveness.[52] This is not a criticism of airpower, far from it. This study's tentative claim is to the effect that each of the five geographically specialized forms of American military power has its unique strengths and limitations. Airpower, thanks to revolutionary improvements in ISR, precision, and stealth, is close to perfection.

The burning issue for the future is not so much the ability to perform yet more immaculately from the sky, but instead to fit that still improving competence into a truly holistic approach to warfare. That approach, in its turn, needs to fit into a genuinely holistic grand strategic approach to war, peace, and deterrence. And the unique geography of a war, terrain in the soldier's worldview, must always offer reasonably distinctive incentives and disincentives to employ airpower in its many aspects for the joint fighting project.

Despite the visions of some of the technophiles among us, the IT revolution will not retire the significance of either politics or physical and cultural geography. This is easy to demonstrate in historical, logical, and common sense terms, but it is not overly helpful to the airpower planner in the twenty-first century. That is why the concluding section of the study must seek to answer the all but unanswerable question directly, "How can America secure the leverage it will need from its predictable airpower advantage?" Some readers may need to be reminded that America's transformed airpower will have to be effective in the face of transformed enemy capabilities and tactics. The defense has not been banished or definitively vanquished.

## Historical Context

In good measure, people and institutions are part prisoners of their pasts and of their interests in the present and the future. The contemporary controversy in the US armed forces over the character of future wars and warfare is amply fuelled by genuine ground for uncertainty. Will the challenge be largely regular or irregular? Is a high-technology-based near-peer challenge a significant source of quite near-term menace, or is it a distant possibility and, for now, a figment more of paranoia than of careful net assessment? And, even as history marches along unpredictably to no predetermined destination, the important details of current controversy are debated in the exceptionally potent historical context of nearly a century of air, land, and sea disagreement over who can and should be allowed to try to do what, by when, at what cost, and with what strategic and political consequences.

The final point just noted tends not to be prominent in American debate. That debate is more comfortable dealing with the difficult enough problems of actual war fighting, let alone venturing higher than the overhead flank into the rarefied zone wherein the political purposes of the fighting in question should dominate discussion. As indicated much earlier, America suffers from a strategy deficit that is a mighty hindrance to leveraging what should be its powerfully multi-faceted airpower advantage. It is not possible to approach the urgent issue of the airpower advantage in future warfare competently in the absence of a firm grasp of airpower's near century-long struggle for organizational influence and independence. America's airpower advocates have sought doctrinal self-determination and the opportunity to demonstrate as much relative influence in warfare as they could squeeze out of other military organizations determined to protect their interests. "Fear, honor, and interest" rule, as always.

## US Airpower Advantage in Future Warfare

This wide ranging study of the probable and possible US airpower advantage in future warfare reaches six major conclusions.

*First, because airpower, broadly defined, is and will long remain a prime source of US asymmetrical advantage, it should be exploited to the fullest for all the leverage it can deliver.* As other concluding points indicate, this will only be possible in the context of a sound theory of warfare overall, which is to say sound for the particular war in question, and an effective joint/integrated strategy, military and nonmilitary. Defenders of the airpower contribution to future warfare, faced with heavy criticism and other doubts deriving from elsewhere in the armed forces, should not be moved to compromise their basic stance. That stance is to insist upon the objective claim that the relative leverage of airpower is recognized to be highly situational. The issue, hence the subject of this study, is the airpower "advantage," not the ability of airpower to deliver decisive military, possibly strategic, and hopefully political victory in all cases. Such an imperial claim does untold harm to the sensible case for airpower's significance. In war and warfare, to the degree feasible, a belligerent should always strive to fight on the most favorable terms it can impose on the enemy. Given America's lead in, indeed identification with, high technology, it would be bizarre, actually impossible, as well as foolish for the country's military planners and strategists not to look for every effective way in which airpower can deliver advantage. Plausible situational objections to some uses of airpower should be acknowledged, and their implications, when practicable, noted, assessed, and employed to modify military behavior.

*Second, many people, including scholars and military professionals, appear to be genuinely confused about the distinction between airpower as a "war winner" and airpower as a "war decider."* Even at the high end of the airpower leverage scale, the distinction matters. In Gulf Wars I and II, in Bosnia, in Kosovo, and in the regular war to depose the Taliban from Kabul, US airpower either decided which side would win or apparently independently provided the leverage for victory. Of course, there are always multiple reasons for success and failure in war, and all claims for relative advantage that strongly privilege one military element—airpower in this case—will be contested.

In some historical cases, certainly in the five recent ones just cited, a key role for airpower was not the only approach that could have been adopted. US and allied landpower, with much less airpower support, could have won or delivered the advantage required in all five conflicts. This is an important but not exactly devastating caveat. After all, strategy is about the choices made among ways, means, and ends.[53] There will usually be alternative theories of how the enemy's will to resist can best be broken. The point is that in these five cases, airpower was employed successfully, if inevitably controversially in some operational terms, to shape the course and outcome of hostilities. But these were wars, or less than wars, of discretion. They were waged to defeat or coerce enemies barely worthy of the title. The situational reality behind this second conclusion will not always be so permissive. Against an enemy cunning in the ways of warfare and able to employ information-led forces, the vital issue of just what should airpower contribute to the joint US effort becomes a topic of outstanding importance. And it will be necessary, though alas not certain, for American strategists to find a correct enough answer rapidly. They will have to be adaptable to the surprises and surprise effects that the bilateral dimension of war always imposes. Today's argument about the future advantage securable through the use of airpower is certain to be tried, though probably not settled definitively, in the actual battlespace of warfare.

*Third, it is futile to debate the subject of America's airpower advantage either strictly from the perspective of rational strategic analysis or even with heavy-to-dominant reference to interorganizational politics and influence in Washington.* It is a fact that high technology is the American way in warfare. It has to be. A high-technology society cannot possibly prepare for, or attempt to fight, its wars in any other than a technology-led manner. A technology privileging American approach to combat is of long standing and is beyond intelligent debate. To seek technology solutions to military challenges, in many cases whether or not there are superior or comparable alternatives theoretically available, is the American style. The reasons for this condition reach back to Colonial times, certainly through the nineteenth century, and became legendary among America's allies and foes in World War II. Since there is an undeniable sense in which the American love affair with machinery is so deep-seated as to be cultural, its strategists must exploit this enduring fact for all it is worth, while seeking, typically with only limited success, to curb its negative influence. When airpower is asked to do too much, this American-preferred leading way in warfare will fail.

*Fourth, as a strategist this author is distressed to find that the long-standing debate over landpower versus airpower is still alive and blooming.* Generally, the debate is phrased carefully, with nuance and nods toward currently acceptable slogans and dogmas, and even with the making of some unavoidable concessions to the adversary's position. But, not far beneath the polite exchange of analyses lies the struggle over who is top dog. Is landpower the supported element or is airpower? This debate would be laughable were it not so serious in the damage it does to the national security. America needs a unified theory of war and warfare, and it has to try to cure itself of its strategic allergy. And yet, stovepipe thinking and behavior continue to thrive. To be fair, the fault does not lie only with the people in uniform. The Constitution has much to answer for. Politicians, not all of whom are strategically literate, find that a much divided military establishment is advantageous for control and constituency benefit. Decisions on policy, strategy, and defense planning are made in an endless and seamlessly complex, even chaotic, process. This political reality can be hard to convey with any approximation to accuracy to those who lack first-hand experience of the phenomenon.

To be crystal clear on the matter, there should be no room for general debate on landpower versus airpower. The advantages of each are almost invariably enhanced by the other and will vary widely from context to context because every conflict must have significantly unique features. But, in all circumstances, the distinctive strengths and limitations of landpower and airpower have to be recognized, especially by those who are most reluctant to do so. The airpower advantage in future warfare cannot be a single story. This is not to deny the radical tactical and operational advances that the past decade has recorded in airpower's potency. Such due recognition, however, must not be permitted to encourage further the unhelpfully military operational, even tacticized, approach to war which has long been dominant in the US way of warfare. The shadows of Napoleon, Lee, Moltke, and Schlieffen still fall heavily upon the American approach to war and warfare.

*Fifth, it is understandably, if often unfortunately, difficult for people to escape capture by the law of their favored instrument.* Airpersons love to fly. That is why they do what they do. As a consequence, it is hard for them to accept the fact that there are significant limitations to the leverage that airpower will deliver, albeit deliver variably in diverse conditions. Anyone whose career is devoted to developing and practicing an extremely demanding, as well as satisfying, technical and tactical mastery is apt to develop a matching worldview. Although one can always find arguments in praise of a deeply favored military agency, a significant source of the opinion will lie with a particular powerful organizational culture. This is a fact, though one rarely admitted.

It is no less a fact, regardless of the strength of the case for airpower being employed as the "leading edge" in a particular conflict, that human beings can only live upon the land. Sir Julian Corbett's much quoted acknowledgment of this only seemingly banal point in his 1911 classic, *Some Principles of Maritime Strategy*, greatly strengthened the confidence with which he has been read by non-sea-minded people.[54] So it should be also on the subject of airpower. No matter how decisive airpower may be in warfare, the purpose of the action can only be to influence political behavior on the land. There can be no other purpose. Air warfare, in common with warfare at sea, in and from space, and through cyberspace, ultimately is meaningless on its own terms. This is an objective fact, inherent in the nature, not the ever changing character, of war.

*Sixth, the only key able to unlock the complete leverage that US airpower can deliver in future warfare is strategy.* Moreover, that strategy must be developed and maintained hierarchically, notwithstanding the multiple dialogs necessary among the levels. Those levels, in descending order, are national security strategy or grand strategy, national military strategy, and strategy for individual conflicts. The character of each conflict and the identity, especially the scope, of US policy goals must shape choices in strategy. They will not determine it fully because strategy is a pragmatic undertaking that will not yield useful advantage if it seeks to direct behavior to perform impractical missions. These words by British strategist Lawrence Freedman can scarcely be bettered for their identification of the heart of the matter. "Strategy constitutes the creative element in any exercise of power. It involves the search for the optimum relationship

34

between political ends and the means available for obtaining them."[55]

Alternatively, one could turn to the perennially relevant pages of Clausewitz's *On War*. But, the United States continues to be hobbled in the leverage it can obtain from its armed forces in peace and war by its seemingly systemic, perhaps cultural, aversion to the sophisticated practice of strategy. And to overcome that aversion, Americans require the services of a holistic theory of war and warfare. Only then will its potential airpower advantage be fully liberated to fly and hit the target.

### Notes

1. I have discussed America's problem with strategy in many places, most recently in *Irregular Enemies and the Essence of Strategy: Can the American Way of War Adapt?* (Carlisle, PA: Strategic Studies Institute, US Army War College, March 2006), pp. 31-2; and *Fighting Talk: Forty Maxims on War, Peace, and Strategy* (Westport, CT: Praeger Security International, 2007). For the purposes of this paper, I choose to define airpower in the minimalist tradition as anything that flies. In this instance, a controversy over definition, far from being simply an exercise in scholasticism, has profound implications for grand and military strategy, as well as for the roles and missions of the services.

2. See Edward N. Luttwak, *Strategy: The Logic of War and Peace*, revised ed. (Cambridge, MA: The Belknap Press of Harvard University Press, 2001), p.188.

3. For two first-rate studies that argue the case for a radical improvement in airpower's competitive position vis-à-vis landpower in regular warfare, see Benjamin S. Lambeth, *The Transformation of American Air Power* (Ithaca, NY: Cornell University Press, 2000); and David E. Johnson, *Learning Large Lessons: The Evolving Roles of Ground Power and Air Power in the Post-Cold War Era*, MG–405–AF (Santa Monica, CA: RAND, 2006).

4. Outstanding treatments of the contrasting world views of the armed services include Carl H. Builder, *The Masks of War: American Military Styles in Strategy and Analysis* (Baltimore, MD: The Johns Hopkins University Press, 1989); and J.C. Wylie, *Military Strategy: A General Theory of Power Control* (1967; Annapolis, MD: Naval Institute Press, 1989), especially Ch. 5.

5. See B.H. Liddell Hart, *Strategy: The Indirect Approach* (1941; London: Faber and Faber, 1967), Ch. 22; and Luttwak, *Strategy*, Ch. 13.

6. The "tacticization of strategy" is discussed helpfully in Michael I. Handel, *Masters of War: Classical Strategic Thought*, 3rd ed. (London: Frank Cass, 2001), pp. 355-60. Handel believes that the advent of air war promoted such tacticization by creating "a situation in which targeting has *de facto* become a substitute for proper strategic planning," p. 358. He claims, not unpersuasively, that "in the twentieth century, particularly after the Second World War, an additional cause [of tacticization] emerged in the form of military-technological developments (i.e.,

35

new military means) that instead of serving strategy in fact determined the logic underlying major strategic choices." Ibid.

7. Michael Evans, *The Continental School of Strategy: The Past, Present and Future of Land Power,* Study Paper No. 305 (Duntroon, ACT, Australia: Land Warfare Studies Centre, 2004), p.84.

8. Carl von Clausewitz, *On War,* edited and translated by Michael Howard and Peter Paret (1832; Princeton, NJ: Princeton University Press, 1976), p.141.

9. Bernard Brodie, *War and Politics* (New York: Macmillan, 1973), p. 452.

10. Lambeth, *Transformation of American Air Power* is now showing its age, but it remains a work of lasting merit.

11. Thucydides, *The Landmark Thucydides: A Comprehensive Guide to "The Peloponnesian War,"* edited by Robert B. Strassler (ca. 400 BC; New York: The Free Press, 1996), p.43.

12. Clausewitz, *On War,* p.75.

13. Wylie, *Military Strategy,* p.72 (emphasis in the original text).

14. Colin S. Gray, *Modern Strategy* (Oxford: Oxford University Press, 1999), pp. 17-23; and *Strategy and History: Essays on Theory and Practice* (London: Routledge, 2006), pp. 1-13, 74-80.

15. See Eliot A. Cohen, *Supreme Command: Soldiers, Statesmen, and Leadership in War* (New York: The Free Press, 2002). This is the latest, but certainly far from the last, commentary on civil-military relations in its relation to strategy.

16. David MacIsaac, "Voices from the Central Blue: The Air Power Theorists," in Peter Paret, ed., *Makers of Modern Strategy: from Machiavelli to the Nuclear Age* (Princeton, NJ: Princeton University Press, 1986), p. 624.

17. Ibid., p. 647.

18. I.B. Holley Jr., "Reflections on the Search for Airpower Theory", in Phillip S. Meilinger, ed., *The Paths of Heaven: The Evolution of Airpower Theory* (Maxwell AFB, AL: Air University Press, 1997), pp. 598-9.

19. Wylie, *Military Strategy,* pp. 33, 36.

20. Frederick W. Kagan, *Finding the Target: The Transformation of American Military Policy* (New York: Encounter Books, 2006), pp. 125-6.

21. Johnson, *Learning Large Lessons,* is essential reading as a historical marker in the debate.

22. Lambeth, *Transformation of American Air Power,* Ch. 7. He continues his politically sensitive narrative and analysis in *Mastering the Ultimate High Ground: Next Steps in the Military Uses of Space* (Santa Monica, CA: RAND, 2003).

23. Keith B. Payne, *The Fallacies of Cold War Deterrence and a New Direction* (Lexington, KY: The University of Kentucky Press, 2001), offers a devastating critique of orthodox deterrence theory and policy.

24. John G. Hines, Ellis M. Mishulovich, and John F. Shull, *Soviet Intentions, 1965-1985,* 2 vols. (McLean, VA: BDM Federal, 22 September 1995), is indispensable.

25. See the recent testimony by Keith B. Payne before the House Armed Services Committee on July 18, 2007. Payne was a principal author of the Bush Administration's NPR.

26. For example, the contemporary health of theory for spacepower can be gauged by a perusal of these brave offerings: Jim Oberg, *Space Power Theory* (Colorado Springs, CO: US Space Command, 2000); Everett C. Dolman, *Astropolitik: Classical Geopolitics in the Space Age* (London: Frank Cass, 2002); and John J. Klein, *Space Warfare: Strategy, Principles and Policy* (London: Routledge, 2006).

27. See Carl H. Builder, *The Icarus Syndrome: The Role of Air Power Theory in the Evolution and Fate of the US Air Force* (New Brunswick, NJ: Transaction Publishers, 1993).

28. Air Chief Marshal Sir Arthur Harris quoted in Sir Charles Webster and Noble Frankland, *The Strategic Air Offensive Against Germany, 1939-1945,* Vol. II (London: Her Majesty's Stationery Office, 1961), p.190. Harris urged this evidence bereft item of faith upon Winston Churchill on November 3, 1943.

29. I probably should plead guilty to some inadvertent promotion of the fallacy that wars are either regular or irregular in character. I tried to warn readers against such a view, but I doubt if my caveat had the potency, it certainly lacked the conceptual expediency, of the binary distinction. See Colin S. Gray, *Another Bloody Century: Future Warfare* (London: Phoenix, 2006), Chs. 5-6.

30. Ibid., Ch. 2. Historian Jeremy Black reminds us that "an understanding of war requires contextualization. Military history exists in a context of other histories." *Rethinking Military History* (London: Routledge, 2004), p.243.

31. See Ian Gooderson, *Air Power at the Battlefront: Allied Close Air Support in Europe, 1943-45* (London: Frank Cass, 1998); and Richard P. Hallion, *Strike from the Sky: The History of Battlefield Air Attack, 1911-1945* (Washington, DC: Smithsonian Institution Press, 1989).

32. Benjamin S. Lambeth provides another of his excellent operational histories in *Air Power Against Terror: America's Conduct of Operation Enduring Freedom* (Santa Monica, CA: RAND, 2005).

33. Larry M. Wortzel, *China's Nuclear Forces: Operations, Training, Doctrine, Command, Control, and Campaign Planning* (Carlisle, PA: Strategic Studies Institute, US Army War College, May 2007), offers a most useful review of recent Chinese professional military literature.

34. Wylie, *Military Strategy*, p.70 (emphasis in the original text).

35. Ibid., p. 72.

36. Eliot A. Cohen, "The Mystique of US Air Power," *Foreign Affairs,* Vol. 73, No. 1 (January-February 1994), pp. 109-24.

37. See Andrew J. Bacevich and Eliot A. Cohen, eds., *War Over Kosovo: Politics and Strategy in a Global Age* (New York: Columbia University Press, 2001); and Benjamin S. Lambeth, *NATO's Air War for Kosovo: A Strategic and Operational Assessment* (Santa Monica, CA: RAND, 2001).

38. Max Boot, "The New American Way of War," *Foreign Affairs,* Vol. 82, No. 4 (July/August 2003), pp. 41-58. A far less excited analysis was offered in Stephen Biddle, *Afghanistan and the Future of Warfare: Implications for Army and Defense* (Carlisle, PA: Strategic Studies Institute, US Army War College, November 2002).

39. Culture is a much contested concept among scholars, especially in regard to its significance for national security. Recent overall reviews of the debate include Lawrence Sondhaus, *Strategic Culture and Ways of War* (London: Routledge, 2006); and Colin S. Gray, "Out of the Wilderness: Prime Time for Strategic Culture," *Comparative Strategy*, Vol. 26, No. 1 (January-February 2007), pp. 1-20. See also John Glenn, Darryl Howlett, and Stuart Poore, eds., *Neorealism Versus Strategic Culture* (Aldershot, UK: Ashgate, 2004); and Theo Farrell, *The Norms of War: Cultural Beliefs and Modern Conflict* (Boulder, CO: Lynne Rienner Publications, 2005). The market for cultural awareness exploded into life in the 2000s when the US armed forces realized that they were trying to influence people in Afghanistan and Iraq who they did not really begin to understand. When one is attempting to change minds, rather than blow them away, local beliefs and attitudes assume high strategic importance. Contemporary American doctrinal publications on COIN are almost over-full of insistence for a cultural perspective. There is some danger that, with all the naïve enthusiasm of the recently converted, the American defense establishment is in the process of settling—briefly—upon cultural expertise as the panacea solution to most of its problems in irregular warfare. See Robert H. Scales, Jr., "Culture-Centric Warfare," *Naval Institute Proceedings*, Vol. 130, No. 10 (October 2004), pp. 32-6. Less dramatic, but more persuasive, was Montgomery McFate, "The Military Utility of Understanding Adversary Culture," *Joint Force Quarterly*, No. 38 (3rd quarter, 2005), pp. 42-8. The fact that Americans today are simply rediscovering two of the most ancient truths about warfare—know the enemy and yourself—does not lessen its significance. Every generation, so it seems, needs to reread Sun-tzu, *The Art of War*, translated by Ralph Sawyer (ca. 400 BC; Boulder, CO: Westview Press, 1994), especially p. 179.

40. Clausewitz, *On War*, p.605.

41. This is the binding argument in Colin S. Gray, *War, Peace, and International Relations: An Introduction to Strategic History* (London: Routledge, 2007).

42. It is open season for geopolitical speculation on the future architecture of balance of power politics. Amidst a drove of interesting studies, well guesses, there is much to recommend C. Dale Walton, *Geopolitics and the Great Powers in the Twenty-first Century: Multipolarity and the Revolution in Strategic Perspective* (London: Routledge, 2007). With ideology retired for a while as a motive force from great-power competition, geopolitics returns to pole position.

43. Amitai Etzioni, *From Empire to Community: A New Approach to International Relations* (Basingstoke, UK: Palgrave Macmillan, 2004). World peace through world community is an intellectually and culturally compelling idea. Alas, it is just too far from contemporary realization to be of much practical interest for policy. With some reluctance I have located some of the weaknesses in the communitarian approach in my "Sandcastle of Theory: A Critique of Amitai Etzioni's Communitarianism," *American Behavioral Scientist*, Vol. 48, No. 12 (August 2005), pp. 1607-25.

44. A former president of the British Association for the Advancement of Science advises that "forecasters have generally failed dismally to foresee drastic changes brought about by completely unpredictable discoveries."

Martin Rees, *Our Final Century: Will Civilization Survive the Twenty-First Century?* (London: Arrow Books, 2003), p.14.

45. The Shanghai Co-operation Organization, which has some potential to serve as a Sino-Russian-led Eurasian counterweight to NATO, held large multinational military maneuvers near Chelyabinsk in Russia in August 2007. The armed forces of Tajikistan, Kyrgyzstan, and Kazakhstan participated, along with Russians and Chinese. This may not mean very much militarily, but it is unquestionably a sign of the times of which the United States has to take due note. Somewhat organized opposition to a US-led world order is beginning to make a showing. See "'Rival to NATO' begins first military exercise," *The Times* (London), 6 August 2007, p.32.

46. See Phillip C. Saunders and Charles D. Lutes, "China's ASAT Test: Motivations and Implications," *Joint Force Quarterly*, No. 46 (3rd quarter, 2007), pp. 39-45. For a usefully broader view, see Andrew Scobell and Larry M. Wortzel, eds., *Shaping China's Security Environment: The Role of the People's Liberation Army* (Carlisle, PA: Strategic Studies Institute, US Army War College, October 2006).

47. Mark Schneider, *The Nuclear Forces and Doctrine of the Russian Federation* (Fairfax, VA: The National Institute Press, for the US Nuclear Strategy Forum, 2006), is a reliable source.

48. Colin S. Gray, *The Sheriff: America's Defense of the New World Order* (Lexington, KY: The University Press of Kentucky, 2004), presents the reasoning for this claim in some detail. I completed *The Sheriff* prior to the invasion of Iraq in 2003, but I have no wish to change my argument. World order requires a policing agent. The fact that the United States performed poorly in Iraq beyond the regime take-down phase does not invalidate the sense in the policy.

49. Barry R. Posen, "Command of the Commons: The Military Foundation of US Hegemony," *International Security*, Vol. 28, No. 1 (Summer 2003), pp. 5-46.

50. I borrow the phrase from Adolf Hitler. In his New Year's message on 1 January 1943 to the Sixth Army, surrounded at Stalingrad, he offered his doomed soldiers the comforting promise that "you can rely on me with rock-like confidence." The moral of this illustration is to the effect that one should always beware of policy makers who speak with a confidence that history does not allow.

51. Clausewitz, *On War,* pp. 566-73.

52. Lambeth, *Transformation of American Air Power.*

53. Harry R. Yarger, *Strategic Theory for the 21st Century: The Little Book on Big Strategy* (Carlisle, PA: Strategic Studies Institute, US Army War College, February 2006), is a fine achievement. I recommend it strongly, even for those who believe themselves to be strategically expert.

54. Julian S. Corbett, *Some Principles of Maritime Strategy* (1911; Annapolis, MD: Naval Institute Press, 1988), p.16.

55. Lawrence Freedman, "Strategic Coercion," in Freedman, ed., *Strategic Coercion: Concepts and Cases* (Oxford: Oxford University Press, 1998), p.14.

www.ingramcontent.com/pod-product-compliance
Lightning Source LLC
Chambersburg PA
CBHW031333290526
45784CB00014B/2622